BROMYARD
VICTORIAN HERITAGE

A Book of Photographs

2005

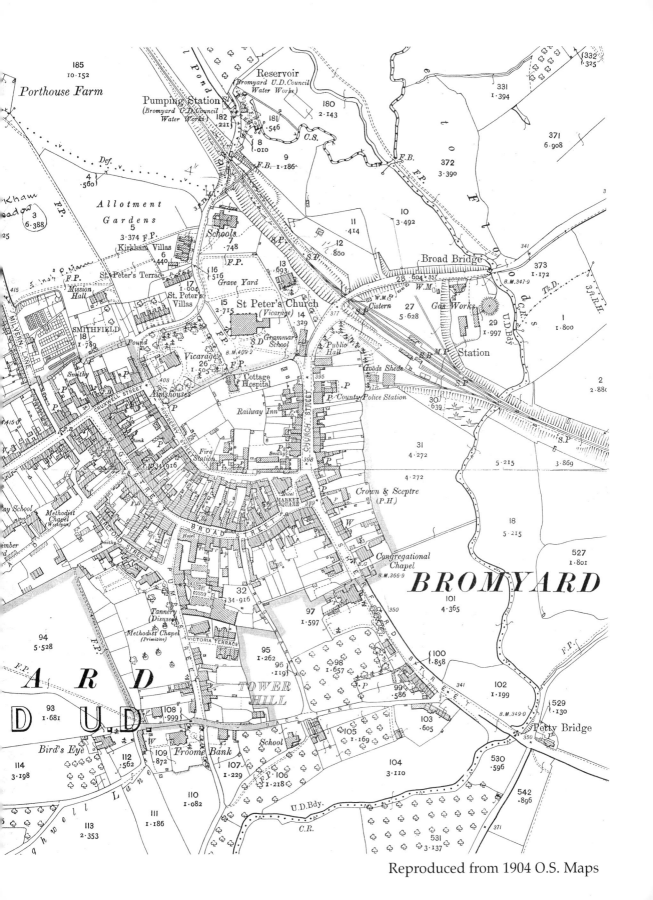

Reproduced from 1904 O.S. Maps

The Bromyard & District Local History Society
5 Sherford Street, Bromyard, HR7 4DL
www.bromyard.historysociety.org.uk

ISBN 0 9546212 0 4

Set in Palatino and printed in Great Britain by
Orphans Press, Leominster, Herefordshire

Cover Illustrations.
Front: Market Square: the old Market House taken down in 1844 (copied from an original painting).

Back: Top: Bromyard 1844 (Geoff Gwatkin)
Bottom: Bromyard 1998 (Geoff Gwatkin)

Title page: A view of Bromyard from the Stourport road in the 1880s.

Other publications of the Bromyard & District Local History Society:

* *Bromyard: A Local History* (1970)
* *Bromyard Parish Registers* by E D Pearson (1974)
* *Bromyard: The Day Before Yesterday* A book of photographs (1979)
Whitbourne: A Bishop's Manor by P Williams (1979)
* *Little Cowarne: A Herefordshire Village* by J Hopkinson (1983)
**Herefordshire Under Arms* by C Hopkinson (1985)
Bromyard: Minster, Manor And Town by P Williams (1987)
* *A Pocketful of Hops.* Hop Growing in the Bromyard Area (1988)
Bromyard: Round And About by D Waller (1991)
Two Churches: Two Communities. St Peter's Bromyard and St James's Stanford Bishop
by E D Pearson (1993)
A History of Bredenbury and its Landed Estate by Jennifer Weale (1997)
Avenbury and the ruined church of St Mary by P Williams (2000)
Where Have All The Courts Gone? A monograph by J Hopkinson (2003)
The Churches of the Bromyard Rural Deanery An Informal Guide by D M Annett (2003)

* OUT OF PRINT

Contents

INTRODUCTION

The Bromyard and District Local History Society, formed in 1966 to research and record the history of the town and its surrounding rural district, has from the beginning collected old photographs. The acquisition of several collections from local residents led to the publication in 1979 of *'Bromyard: the day before yesterday'*, a book of photographs covering the period 1880-1920. This has been out of print for some years and we were encouraged, when planning the Victorian Exhibition in 2004, to consider a replacement.

This new book covers roughly the same period and concentrates on the development of the town. It does not cover the First World War which we felt needed its own history. We have used many of the same photographs, but not always in the same context. Some of the prints date back to the 1860s, some are prints from glass negatives which are less than perfect and a few have suffered some wear and tear, but they have been included because we feel the information they present is valuable. The majority were taken at the end of the 19th century when the hand-held camera made photography a popular activity. Local postcards also became available at this time and we have included some of these. There are no studio photographs and, regrettably, only one interior.

The tour of Bromyard with which the book begins covers an area only very slightly larger than the white area of the 1844 map on the back cover. Apart from the changes caused by the building of the 1967 by-pass, the street pattern shown has remained the same to the present day, although some buildings have been demolished and replaced and some streets have different names. Broad Street in 1905 looks very like Broad Street in 2005 even with the Falcon Hotel covered in plaster.

In contrast to this stability some of the major 19th century developments have left few traces. The railway, so important for Bromyard's business life during the period of this book, closed in the 1960s and the site is now a trading estate. The two gas-works which supplied the town with gas for more than a hundred years from 1856 have both disappeared, the earlier building during the construction of the by-pass, and the later one when the site was sold in the early 1960s. The house built for the manager of the gas-works can still be seen near Broadbridge. More important than these, the market closed in the 1970s, leaving only the traces described on Page 22. Bromyard had held markets for a thousand years, a necessary hub for the surrounding district before modern transport allowed people to travel more widely.

In the transport section of the book we have also travelled, using photographs taken in the town where possible, but adding others from the wider area when necessary.

When *'Bromyard: the day before yesterday'* was published there were still some residents who were born during the reign of Queen Victoria. This is not the case today and our information must come from other sources. The Society's holdings are substantial and constantly updated, but there are gaps. If any reader knows where we can obtain a 19th century photograph of the racecourse or the Friends Meeting house we shall be delighted.

Exploring the Town

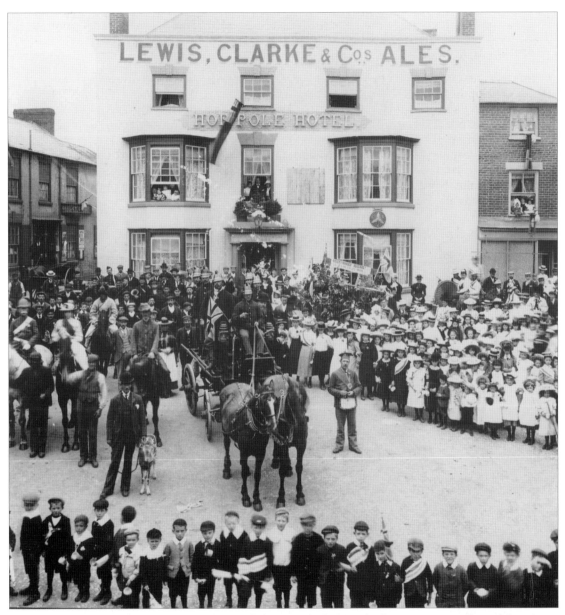

We begin in the Market Square, in front of the Hop Pole Hotel, always a centre for celebrations. This is a photograph of Pretoria Day, 5 June 1900, a British victory in the Boer War in South Africa. The firemen in their helmets, on the wagon, indicate that this is the horse-drawn fire engine. The goat was the regimental mascot of the Herefordshire Rifles. It was fortunate that Pretoria was taken because the plans for the celebration had been made well in advance.

In this early view of the Square, only the Post Office had a Victorian shop window, to the right of the door. It was also a stationers and printers and from 1861 was kept by Mrs Margaret Bennett.

In the early 1900s the Bennett family were still at the Post Office, Mr Benjamin Palmer had transformed the building to the right and there was a new gas streetlamp. Across the road the drapers had been rebuilt and the Misses Johnson, also stationers, were selling postcards.

The old Market House shown on the front of this book was removed in 1844. A new market building had been erected on the corner of Rowberry Street and Church Street but the traders continued to use the Square. Market Day was changed from Monday to Thursday in 1878. The photograph above was taken when Frederick Perkins still had his business in Cruxwell Street where, according to his daughter, the busiest time was on Sunday mornings. Below he can be seen standing in the doorway of the shop on the corner of the Square, to which he had moved. He continued to trade there until the building was demolished in the 1930s to widen the road.

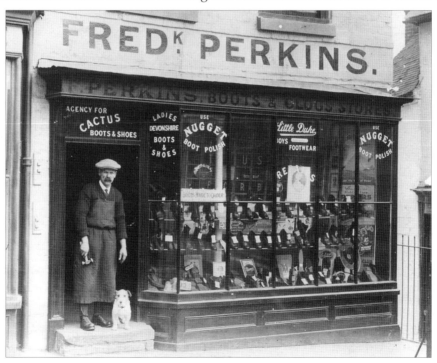

In 1898 Mr and Mrs Albert Pettifer came from Wiltshire as newly-weds to open an ironmonger's shop in Broad Street. They also sold and repaired bicycles, but Albert's real interest was in cars and he bought his first car, a Benz, in 1898. The shop is now Olive's, a haberdashery and wool shop, run by Mrs Olive Allsup.

A few years later the sign above Pettifer's advertises the motor depot and garage which were behind the shop in Rowberry Street (see p 53). The next door shop with the sun blind was a tailor's and gents' outfitters, also owned by Mr Pettifer.

A very impressive display of harness outside the saddlers in Broad Street in the 1890s. George Ward had been a saddler here for many years, before the Baggotts. This is thought to be where Gilbert's greengrocer's shop now is.

Two views of Market Day outside the Falcon around 1900. Farmers' wives brought their eggs, butter and poultry to sell from the pavement. A live hen and a duck can be seen on the left.

Past the group of people in the lower photograph are the buildings on the corner of High Street and Pump Street which were soon to be dramatically changed (see p10).

A backward glance from the Falcon Hotel. Opposite the Falcon is the Lion Inn; both are timber-framed buildings, then covered in plaster. Past the Falcon can be seen the two shoe shops, Stead and Simpson and Lloyd's, later Ross. Beyond Frog Lane is the splendid new shop front of Powell and Co.'s Progress Stores replacing the windows shown below.

In Pump Street the first building on the left is the tannery. Next door is Tan House, home of the tanner James Jenks, where Sunday School classes and Wesleyan Methodist services were held. Beyond the houses is the low wall in front of the new Primitive Methodist Chapel built in 1899 (see p 30)

Workmen in the tannery c.1890.

Looking up Pump Street, Tower House is seen before the stucco was removed to reveal the fine timber framing. Charles I is said to have stayed here. It is thought that the mediaeval stones in the gateposts came from Bromyard Church when an early gate there was dismantled.

Across from Tower House and looking back towards the tannery, the cottages which were demolished to make way for the new Primitive Methodist Church are seen behind the trees on the right. The nearer cottages were demolished to create a gap for the new by-pass. Towering over all, the tannery chimney is on the extreme right.

EXPLORING THE TOWN

Oak House, on the corner of Pump Street and High Street, is now HSBC (Midland Bank). Adjoining is the new house and butcher's shop built in 1900 for Mr John James. Next door the house, which was occupied by the High School for Girls before their move to Sherford House in 1898, has been converted for business use by Mr Alfred Newbold, a builder and contractor.

Further up High Street the Bay Horse Inn is set back on the left. On the right the barber stands beneath his pole.

10

James Whitsey Williams came from Worcester to establish his grocer's shop in 1845. This proved very successful and he rebuilt the shop at the end of the century, displaying his name on the parapet. The business which also dealt in seeds, corn and coal, was continued by his son Francis Whitsey Williams, his grandson Raymond Whitsey Williams and great grandson Noel Whitsey Williams before it finally closed. The grocery was sold in 1942-3, but the other businesses continued until 1970.

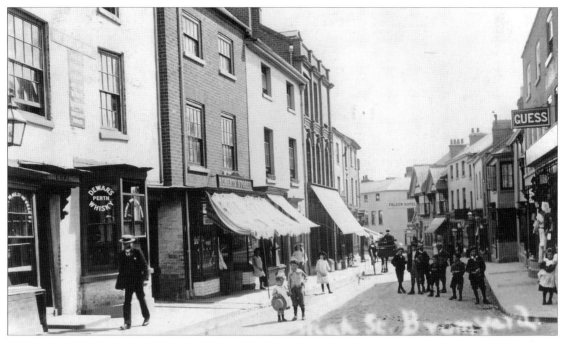

Looking back along High Street from the corner of New Road, beyond the Queen's Arms and Roberts Stores is another tall brick building built in 1893 by Henry Pumphrey for his expanding drapery business.

These young dressmakers worked on the second floor in 'a light and cheery room, well ventilated and well warmed'.

Looking up New Road the warehouse on the left was part of the premises occupied by Mr Donald McIntosh, a draper and general outfitter in the late 19th century. Further up on the right is the Wesleyan Methodist Chapel, built in 1857.

The lower photograph is from the other direction, with the chapel the second building on the left and the Rose & Lion just visible on the right. Note the telegraph pole and wires, erected in the mid 1870s.

Mr Guess, who kept the shop on the corner of New Road, took over the premises and business of Mr McIntosh in 1901. On the left is the shop front of William Box, seen in the lower photograph with his wife in the 1890s. Mr Box was a plumber and decorator.

On the extreme right, and up to the corner of Cruxwell Street, is what is said to be the oldest and most important domestic building in Bromyard. Originally one dwelling, it was split into three and has in later years been converted for trade purposes. The ancient structure is now completely hidden. Two doors down, just beyond the group of children, was Edmund Williams' shop. Here, just after the turn of the century, he sold bicycles and, later, motor-cycles and cars. He designed his own machine, the Edwell motor-cycle. A keen photographer, he took a number of the photographs in this book.

Looking up Sheep Street (now Old Road) from Cruxwell Street on a wet and muddy day. On the right, on the corner of Milvern Lane (now Tenbury Road) is the White Horse public house. Here some timber framed houses have not been hidden behind plaster.

The lower photograph shows a group of smiling gentlemen, evacuated from the White Horse to watch the photographer at work.

The Davidson family and their assistant stand outside their grocery shop in Cruxwell Street. Mr Davidson was also a licensed game dealer, while Mrs Davidson kept a newsagents shop in High Street. This building is now part of the Anchor Cafe.

This is Milvern Lane looking back to the junction with Cruxwell Street and Sheep Street. The picturesque cottages suffered from lack of drains and poor water supply and they were demolished in the 1930s.

The cattle market was off the Tenbury Road. Before that, animals were sold in the streets; cattle in the High Street and New Road, sheep and goats in Sheep Street (now Old Road). Cattle stood loose, guarded by their owners, but pens for sheep and pigs were kept in the White Horse yard and erected every market day. This must have presented a considerable challenge to cleanliness, and gradually during the 19th century the stock markets moved into more enclosed quarters.

Mr Edward Sampson was the founder of Bromyard Smithfield market, behind the White Horse, and first held fortnightly sales there in 1890. In 1893 Bentley, Hobbs and Mytton opened their 'New Market of Bromyard' further north along the lane; the surface of sloping brickwork and gullies is still visible on the ground in front of the industrial building between the Conquest Theatre and the Co-op store: the auctioneers' names can still be seen on the wall of the Co-op car park. Sampson sold out to Mr Ralph Knight in 1899 and the two firms continued to operate on the same day of the week for some years. Later Mr Knight introduced annual horse sales.

The photograph above shows Mr Knight's yard in the early 1900s. The coming of the railway gave a boost to the livestock markets. Bentley, Hobbs & Mytton timed their opening sale on 21 September 1893 to commence on the arrival of the 12.15 pm train. After a successful May stock sale in 1900, a special train with eighteen cattle trucks left Bromyard for Worcester at 10.00pm. However, moving stock at the end of the day by walking them through the streets had not ended by the 1930s.

Angel Place in Cruxwell Street, facing High Street, was demolished in 1957. William Sanders, a tailor, had his home and shop in the house on the left. His son John, born there in 1902, described the house and that of his neighbour as being very heavily timbered. Mr William Chambers had his veterinary surgery at the back of the building on the right in 1890. By 1895 Mr T J Foulkes had taken over and remained there until the 1930s.

By 1909 Mr Charles Powis was the landlord of the Green Dragon, a few yards down Cruxwell Street. Here he is with his wife and two customers. The building was taken down in 1960. The site of all these vanished buildings was used as a car park and, later, for the Leisure Centre. This was expanded in 2004 into the multi-purpose Bromyard Centre, incorporating a new library and information service.

In Rowberry Street we pause to look back towards Cruxwell Street and the trees bordering the vicarage gardens, while the young man and his dog gaze solemnly towards the camera.

The cottage hospital in the Schallenge opened in 1869 with beds for five patients. Supported by public subscriptions it was available to residents within seven miles of Bromyard. It was extended in 1887 and again in 1897 and is shown here in its final form. The hospital closed in 1917 and is now a private house.

In the early 1860s the pub on the left of Church Street was the Three Horseshoes kept by Mr Edward Moss, a blacksmith. The grammar school is at the far end of the street on the left; at that time the only grammar school building.

The later photograph shows a much tidier street. Building has continued along the right hand side. A new magistrates' court was built in 1863 and an adjacent police station and house in 1875. On the left the Three Horseshoes has become the Bell Inn and the imposing house is Fairview, home of Mr Pettifer from 1913 until his death in 1934.

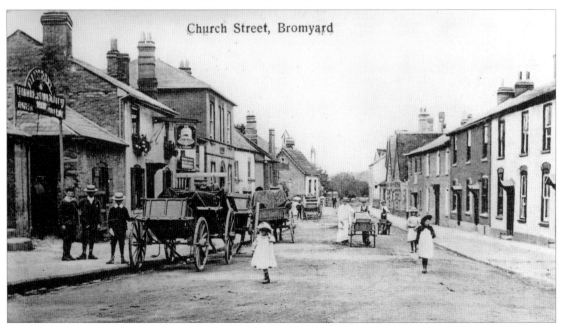

Church Street, Bromyard

The upper photograph looks at Church Street from the other direction. On the left is the decorative brickwork of the magistrates' court. The pub opposite, which had had a number of names over the years, was re-named the Railway Inn in 1877 when the railway line between Bromyard and Worcester was completed. It has retained the name since the line closed but is now a private house. The timber-framed house in the distance is the Bible House, home of the Addymans whose family grocery in the Square traded from 1879 to 1975. Below we see Mr James Addyman outside the house. Note that he was also agent for Phoenix Insurance.

Looking down Sherford Street, the furthest building on the left was the parish lock-up, built in 1844. Seepage from the neighbouring graveyard caused its closure in 1872. The photographer seems to have lost the attention of the bystanders; had the couple driving past upset the cattle?

For travellers to Bromyard from Worcester the Bridge Inn at the bottom of Sherford Street would be a welcome sight. Built in the sixteenth century it traded as an inn until the 1870s and later became a private house.

Churches and Chapels

Our earliest photograph of St Peter's Church was taken in 1863 by Henry Hughes, a local photographer and hairdresser. This view from the north-west looks across the graveyard which by 1906 had space for only forty more graves. A new cemetery was consecrated in 1914.

The handsome vicarage was built about 1800 by Dr George Cope, the vicar 1793-1822, for £1200. It remained in use until 1965 when it became the offices of the Bromyard Rural District Council. A new vicarage was built in part of the garden.

The Rev William Martin, vicar 1877-1913, at the south door of the church. Above the doorway the two carvings, of St Peter holding the keys and of the cross, are thought to be from an earlier church, possibly Saxon. The door has now been replaced and the gates removed but the gate hangers remain. It was during Mr Martin's time that major restoration took place, between 1886 and 1912.

In 1912 the replacement of the old box pews, above, by the new ones, below, was a modernisation in more ways than one. Over a hundred years earlier the vast majority of the old pews had been allocated to local properties, but as these changed hands or were demolished many pews were unused. When the new pews were installed this system lapsed and all seating was free.

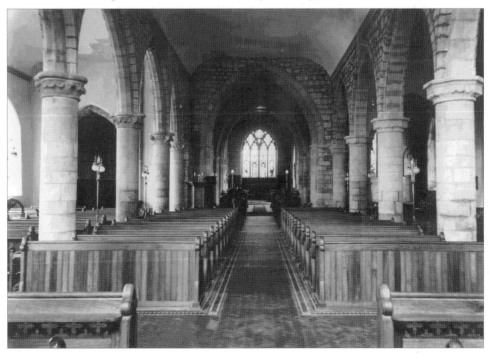

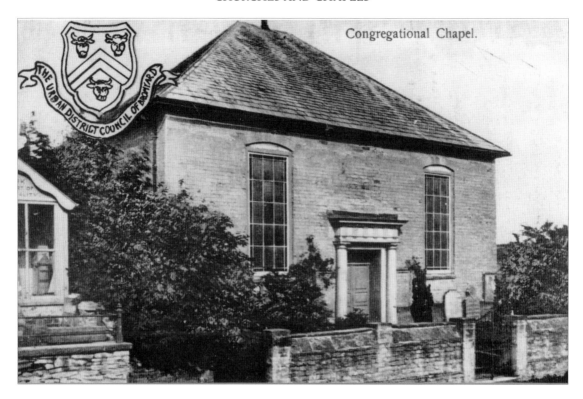

Congregational Chapel.

The Congregational Chapel, built in 1702 in Sherford Street, was the earliest nonconformist chapel in Bromyard and known originally as the Independent Chapel. It was noted in the 1851 Religious Census that 'when really full' it could hold 300 people. In 1869 when the Rev John Peter Jones was minister, the chapel was repaired, six new windows were put in and two new schoolrooms built for the Sunday Schools. The manse behind the chapel, in which the minister lived, was partially rebuilt in 1874. After more restoration in 1892 and reseating in 1922, the chapel remained in use until the 1970s.

The Urban District Council, formed in 1894, obviously thought the building handsome enough to use on a postcard.

The Society of Friends, (Quakers) formed a group in Bromyard in 1668. After meeting for many years in different private houses in the town, a Meeting House was built in the early 18th century; the date 1726 was carved on a windowsill. The building was behind the present shoe shop at 16 Broad Street. During the 18th century members suffered greatly from fines levied for not paying their tithes to the established church. There were never very many Friends – perhaps the tithe issue discouraged them. According to the 1851 Religious Census only four Friends attended the Meeting on March 31st.

Between 1850 and 1872 the Meeting House was used as a schoolroom for the British School, established by the Nonconformists led by James Jenks the tanner.

This photograph was taken shortly before the building was demolished in the 1970s.

Primitive Methodism became very popular during Queen Victoria's reign. The simple building on Tower Hill (above) opened in 1836, was both chapel and manse. In 1851 the attendance figures on the day of the Religious Census were 29 in the morning and 21 in the afternoon, with 25 scholars at each service. At the harvest festival in 1890 both the chapel and a tent outside were packed and people were turned away. The much needed new chapel was built in Pump Street in 1899 (below left).

When the new chapel was opened the whole of the old building was transformed into the new manse, with impressive alterations on the front. This is now two separate dwellings, 4 & 6 Highwell Lane.

The Bromyard Primitive Methodist mission also spread to Bringsty. At first they had nowhere permanent to worship, and often met in the open air, until the chapel was built in 1861.

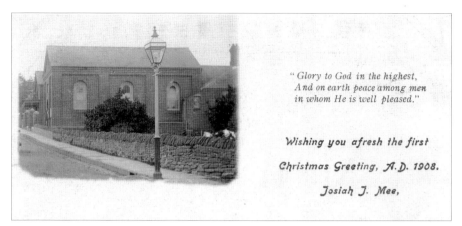

"*Glory to God in the highest,
And on earth peace among men
in whom He is well pleased.*"

Wishing you afresh the first

Christmas Greeting, A.D. 1908.

Josiah J. Mee,

Wesleyan Methodism came to Bromyard in 1825. Two notable Bromyard men, James Jenks, the tanner, and James Whitsey Williams, the grocer, became strong supporters. From 1841 services were held at the Tan House in Pump Street, the home of Mr Jenks, where as many as a hundred people could gather.

The Methodist Chapel in New Road was opened in 1857. It was known for many years as Jenk's Chapel. The first minister, Rev C Williams, was appointed in 1862. The minister in 1908, Josiah Jobson Mee used a photograph of the chapel for his Christmas greeting.

The front porch was added in 1911 and the lower photograph was taken to record the opening. In recent years a new small chapel has been built at the rear and the 1857 building is now used for meetings and classes.

A Roman Catholic Mass was held in Bromyard in 1889, the first time for over 300 years. Temporary locations were used at first until Father Denys Mathieu, who had been a monk at Buckfast Abbey for twenty years, was appointed Catholic priest in 1908. He raised the money to build the first St Joseph's Church in Frog Lane which was opened in 1914.

Father Denys designed the church in Frog Lane and took a major part in the actual work of the building which began in 1913. He was 'a man of many resources, a member of the Society of Inventors of France, a gold medallist of the city of Paris, an expert electrician and an accomplished painter in oils. To raise funds towards the building of the church, he gave French lessons, repaired clocks and made crystal sets'.

St Joseph's Church in Frog Lane was built of reinforced concrete. It remained in use from 1914 until the new church was built in the Old Road in 1957. The seating illustrated in the photograph below was moved to the new church.

Some Schools

Queen Elizabeth I granted a charter for a grammar school in Bromyard in 1566. The original schoolroom is on the left and the new 1894 building on the right. Numbers were never high and the photograph below probably shows the whole school. It became co-educational in January 1914 by uniting with the Girls' High School, and in 1969 it merged with the Secondary Modern School to become the Queen Elizabeth High School on the new site at Ashfields.

A house was built in 1897 to provide accommodation for the headmaster of the grammar school and boys who wished to board. Later some rooms were used for classes and the head retreated to a flat on the top floor. The whole building was converted into flats in the late 1990s.

Bromyard schoolchildren parading down the High Street, probably around 1910.

St Peter's School was built in 1862 from the designs of F R Kempson at a cost of £1250. It was a National (Church of England) school for boys and girls. In 1883 it was transferred to the Education Department and became known as Bromyard Board School. In 1889 the average cost of educating one child for a year was £2.9s.2d.

The staff shown below were teaching the girls and infants at St Peter's after the boys had moved to Linton Lane, the former British (Nonconformist) School.

The Bromyard High School for Girls was started in 1893 in the house in the High Street which is now Pettifers. In 1898 it moved to Sherford House where the girls are seen above with their tennis rackets and below, in their best dresses, inside the building.

Miss E M Martin, the principal of the High School for Girls is seated with other members of staff in the garden of Sherford House. The school closed in 1906.

Another school, named Bromyard Girls' High School, opened in 1910 in the premises formerly occupied by the Ladies College in Tower Hill House on the extreme right. It was this school which united with the grammar school in 1914.

Toll Houses

The Turnpike Act of 1751 enabled trustees to build toll houses on the main roads from Bromyard in order to obtain funds to keep the roads in repair.

1751 toll charges

"for every coach, chariot, landau, berlin, chaise or calash drawn by four horses etc.	1/-
As above drawn by two horses etc.	6d.
For every waggon, wain, cart or carriage drawn by six draught horses, oxen or beasts of draught	2/-
As above drawn by five horses etc.	1/6d
For every drove of oxen, cows, calves, neats	10d. per score

After the coming of the railways much long distance traffic was transferred to rail and tolls declined. Many trusts were dissolved before 1888 when the newly created county councils assumed responsibility for the roads.

The first three toll houses shown still had their gates when these photographs were taken. Above is the Milvern Lane toll house on the road to Tenbury. The caged bird outside was to warn of approaching traffic.

The Broad Bridge toll house on the Stourport road which is close to the present cemetery gates.

The Petty Bridge toll house which can still be seen beside the Worcester road.

The Piccadilly toll house stood at the junction of the road to Hereford.

This toll house stood at Flaggoner's Green until the 1960s.

Transport

Before the age of the car, horses were the main mode of transport, especially for country people. A good cob or pony could serve many purposes.

Mr Bemand and his son Tom at Grendon Bishop.

Mr Jones in his gig at Goodships Farm, Avenbury. His son Sam stands at the horse's head.

A donkey, if well trained, can be useful for taking children for a ride. In the photograph above Dennis and Miles Belville are about to set off from Tedstone Court. Below, Humphrey Cook of Linceter and Jenny the donkey are taking Lucy and Jim Vernalls to school.

Here the horse waits patiently with the milk cart at the gates of the Schallenge in Rowberry Street.

The Bringsty postman is about to set off after clearing the letter box in the wall of the Brockhampton estate at Clater.

Rev. H G Morgan kept this splendid turnout at the rectory at Stoke Lacy. His son, later known as 'H F S' when he started to build the famous Morgan three-wheeler cars, is on the pony.

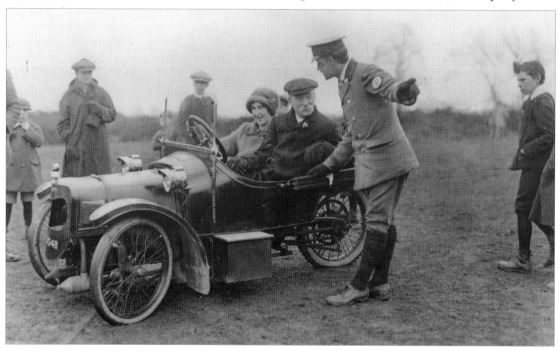

The rector and his daughter Dorothy have arrived at a car rally in Malvern in 1914 in one of the early Morgan cars.

By the Edwardian period the steam engine had been adapted for many different tasks in the country. The upper photograph is of the yard of C & J Smith, haulage and agricultural contractors, The Tiffins, Stoke Lacy, and shows a number of stationary threshing engines and threshers, preparing for work in the 1910s.

Bromyard Queen Nance was a Fowler steam traction engine, built in Leeds in 1909. It worked around Bromyard for many years, at one time in the ownership of Mr Jack Smith of C & J Smith; he donated this photograph of the engine towing a load of shoddy along Old Road. Mr Smith stands beside the engine which is driven by Mr Bracster of Roxpole, Stoke Lacy, who was killed in the Great War.

The steam road roller was a common sight on the roads for decades. Here is the repair gang at work on the Avenbury Lane in the early years of the 20th century. The stones were watered and rolled in; it was to be many years before country lanes were surfaced with tarmacadam.

Steam power was also used in the construction of the railway through Bromyard. The excavator was driven by a steam donkey and was commonly known as the 'steam navvy'. Three were used in the stretch of line between Bromyard and Steens Bridge.

Two views of Bromyard station during its heyday early in the 20th century. The line to Worcester opened in 1877 and that to Leominster in 1897. The latter closed first in 1952 as no longer economic, and the Worcester connection in 1964, as a result of the Beeching report of March 1963.

The introduction of the railway did not see the end of the horse for many more years. Horse-drawn vehicles were still needed to take goods and passengers to and from the station.

A look at the train timetable for March 1905 (from the Bromyard News & Record 23.3.1905) shows five trains daily between Leominster and Worcester. There were connections to London, Hereford, Shrewsbury, Wolverhampton and Birmingham.

LOCAL TIME TABLE

WORCESTER to BROMYARD and LEOMINSTER.

		a.m.	a.m.	p.m.	p.m.	p.m
WORCESTER (Shrub Hill)	d	8.20	10.30	2.38	5.15	7.50
(Foregate-st).		8.23	10.33	2.43	5.18	7.53
Henwick		8.28	10.38	2.48	5.23	7.58
Leigh Court		8.38	10.48	2.58	5.33	8.8
Knightwick		8.46	10.56	3.6	5.41	8.16
Suckley		8.51	11.1	3.11	5.46	8.21
BROMYARD	a	9.2	11.12	3.22	5.57	8.32
,,	d	9.5	11.15	3.25	6.0	8.35
Rowden Mill		9.12	11.22	3.32	6.7	8.42
Fencote		9.22	11.33	3.41	6.18	8.53
Steens Bridge		9.30	11.41	3.51	6.26	9.1
LEOMINSTER	a	9.37	11.48	4.0	6.33	9.8

From LEOMINSTER to BROMYARD and WORCESTER.

LEOMINSTER	d	7.20	8.55	12.10	4.10	7.45
Steens Bridge		7.30	9.5	12.20	4.20	7.55
Fencote		7.41	9.21	12.31	4.31	8.6
Rowden Mill		7.47	9.27	12.37	4.37	8.12
BROMYARD	a	7.54	9.34	12.44	4.44	8.19
,,	d	7.59	9.37	12.47	4.47	8.35
Suckley		8.10	9.48	12.57	4.58	8.46
Knightwick		8.14	9.52	1.1	5.2	8.50
Leigh Court		8.21	9.59	*1.8	5.9	8.57
Henwick		8.31	10.9	1.18	5.19	9.7
WOR'STER (FS)	a	8.35	10.12	1.21	5.22	9.10
,, (SH)	a	8.40	10.17	1.26	5.27	9.15

2 BROMYARD to OXFORD, LONDON &c,

BROMYARD	d	8.55	9.37	12.47	4.47	8.40

HOP-PICKERS AT BROMYARD STATION.

Special trains were run for local events such as the races on the downs, but they were seen more regularly at harvest time when hop-picker specials brought – and returned – several thousand families from the Black Country. The families were carried to the farms on wagons.

While the trains could move people in vast numbers, the cycle gave to individuals a new freedom to travel. These two delightful photographs both come from local collections, but the cyclists and their machines are unfortunately not identified.

The earliest Morgan three-wheelers were built by 'H F S' Morgan at the rectory at Stoke Lacy. As production became established, and before finally moving to Malvern Link, many parts were manufactured in Bromyard by Pettifers. This car, CJ743, is a 1912/13 Morgan Runabout, here seen fitted with a huge acetylene headlamp.

Edmund Williams and his wife and daughter are comfortably settled in the family Reo (1906/7).

Alfred Pettifer with his staff and fleet of cars outside his garage in Rowberry Street rebuilt in 1906 after fire had destroyed the old one the previous summer.

Pettifer's had several contracts with the Royal Mail for van deliveries in the county. This van, on a Darracq chassis, was built in the Bromyard workshop.

Essential Services

FIRE

Fire in towns built largely of wood and plaster with thatched roofs was one of the most feared events and all towns kept fire-fighting equipment.

For many years the fire insurance companies paid for local brigades but these were only expected to attend to fires in premises covered by their companies. In Bromyard this was to cause a lengthy argument over compensation after the 1886 fire which destroyed two houses and damaged four adjoining premises, killing one man.

This engine was the first appliance used in Bromyard. It is believed to have been built in 1766, but it survived into the 20th century. It was normally drawn by two men who then worked a pump handle on each side of the vehicle. The man at the right is said to be Mr Reuben Philpotts, a fireman in the 1920s.

In 1870 a horse-drawn engine was acquired by the town, but sometimes, while the horses were being found, caught and harnessed, the firemen themselves would pull the engine.

The perennial problem in Bromyard was an irregular water supply. In 1850 the public supply was restricted to three or four pumps, which were locked at night, and even the use of private wells was insufficient to cope with the demands of the fire brigade.

After years of disagreement over offers by Mr Phipps of Buckenhill, in 1901 the scheme to pump water from Three Mills (above), supplied from the estate spring, to the reservoir tank at Flaggoner's Green, was implemented and served Bromyard for sixty years.

The disposal of effluent remained a problem as Bromyard expanded and the River Frome remained the ultimate sewer until 1964.

Here we show Bromyard's water benefactor, Mr Richard Phipps of Buckenhill. Bromyard had other reasons to thank Mr Phipps. He gave generously to the restoration of St Peter's Church; he provided a mission hall and hostel for the navvies working on the Leominster railway, and he built the Victoria Temperance Hotel and café in Cruxwell Street. He died in 1910.

The Bromyard Gas Light Company was formed in 1856 and operated from the small gabled building at the bottom of Sherford Street shown on the left.

In 1886 The Bromyard Gas Light Company reported that 'there is an increased use of gas for cooking and heating and .... there are now eight cooking, four boiling and five heating stoves in use'. By 1889 there were 33 street lamps – but these were only used between October and April, and not for three days on each side of a full moon.

However, after complaints about the quality and price of gas, a new company, the Bromyard Gas Light and Power Company was formed in 1893. The new gas works, shown below during a flood in 1912, was built close to the railway station. But Bromyard was still not happy and complaints about the quality, and the lack of lighting when there was a moon, were still being aired in 1910. The 'new' gas works closed at the end of the 1950s.

In 1842 the Parish Constables Act provided for new Superintendent Constables to be appointed at a salary of £70 per year, with an allowance of £20 for 'purchase and upkeep of a horse'. They were also provided with a lock-up house, uniform and equipment.

Bromyard's lock-up below the Congregational church in Sherford Street was built in 1844, but by 1872 unpleasant seepage from the graveyard had rendered it unsatisfactory and it was sold. Dumbleton Hall, in Church Street, where earlier magistrates' courts had been held, was used as a temporary police station until the new Police Station and house were built in 1875 next to the 1863 Magistrates' Court. By this time the Herefordshire Constabulary had been established with Bromyard one of nine divisions.

The photograph above would have been taken about 1890 shortly after the helmet was introduced. Superintendent Ovens sitting in the place of honour, centre front, retired in 1891.

Sport and Recreation

Bromyard is lucky to have the Downs. At various times they were used for horse racing, golf, shooting and bowls. The rifle butts were probably used for practice by the local Volunteers. The race-course was laid out at the end of the Napoleonic Wars as relief work for returning soldiers and the unemployed. There was one meeting each year with races on the flat as well as over hurdles and fences.

BROMYARD HUNT MEETING

FRIDAY, MAY 23RD, 1884,

UNDER GRAND NATIONAL HUNT RULES.

STEWARDS.

THE RIGHT HON. THE EARL OF COVENTRY,   SIR J. R. BAILEY, BART, M.P.   MAJOR RANKIN, M.P. M.F.H.
MAJOR BROWNE, M.F.H.   MICHAEL BIDDULPH, ESQ., M.P.   ANDREW KNOWLES, ESQ., M.F.H.   F. AMES, ESQ., M.F.H.

MR. P. W TAYLOR, (Merryfield,) CHAIRMAN OF COMMITTEE.   MR. H. SCARLETT DAVIES, HON SEC. and TREASURER.
MR. T. ALLIES, CLERK OF THE COURSE and HANDICAPPER.   MR. WALTER CULLIS, JUDGE and CLERK OF THE SCALES.
MR. J. W. HININGS, STARTER.   MR. A. S. ALLEN, STAKEHOLDER.

OAKLEY'S OFFICIAL AND CORRECT LIST.

PUBLISHED UNDER THE SANCTION OF THE COMMITTEE.

2 0 | THE HEREFORD HUNT HURDLE RACE,

Of 22 Sovs. for Hunters that have never won 50 sovs at any one time. Four-year-olds, 11st.; five-year-olds, 11st. 10lbs.; six and aged, 12st. Winners of any race once, 4lbs.; twice, 7lbs. Five-year-olds and upwards that have never won a race, allowed 7lbs. Entrance, 2 sovs each to go to the fund. Distance, about two miles over eight flights of hurdles.

1.—Mr. H. U. Taylor's *Highland Lad* late *Ross*, ...gold body, dark blue sleeves, and black cap
2.—Mr. E. C. Ainsworth's bro m *Flirt*, aged.....magenta and black cap
3.—Mr. H. Mills's *In Bounds*, 5 yrs.........black body, and white sleeves
4.—Mr. E. J. Lewis's bay g *Bonnie Joey*, 4 yrs...green, crimson & black stripes
5.—Mr. John Rogers's *Pirate*, 6 yrs............. scarlet and black cap
6.—Mr. G. H. Shepherd's *Albatrusse*, 5 yrs ...chocolate & yellow sleeves

2 45 | THE BROXASH HUNTERS HURDLE RACE.

Of 25 Sovs. for first horse and 5 Sovs. for second horse. For Hunters that have been regularly hunted with the North and South Hereford, Ledbury, Croome, Worcester, and Ludlow Hounds, and have been the property of the nominator before the 1st of January, 1884. Four-year-olds, 11st.; five-year-olds, 11st. 7lbs.; six and aged, 12st. Winners of £40, once, 7lbs.; twice of £40 or once of £60, 10lbs. extra. Distance, about two-and-a-half miles over ten flights of hurdles. Entrance, 2 sovs to go to the fund.

1.—Mr. T. L. Walker's ch m by Lord Berkley, dam by Old Hereford, aged scarlet and black cap
2.—Mr F. R. Pinkett's *Pinfire*,...............canary, blue sleeves, & cap

4 30 | THE WORCESTER HURDLE RACE,

Of 21 Sovs for Hunters that have never won a race. Four-year-olds, 10st. 7lbs. five-year-olds, 11st. 7lbs.; six and aged, 12st. Distance, two miles over eight flights of hurdles. Entrance, one sov. to go to the fund.

1.—Mr. T. L. Walker's c m by Lord Berkley, dam by Old Hereford, aged scarlet and black cap
2.—Mr. T. E. Williams's *Dubious*, by Speculative, dam Red Wine, yrs. blue jacket, red cap
3.—Mr. H. U Taylor's *Highland Lad*, late Ross 4 yrs.....gold body dark blue sleeves and black cap
4.—Mr. E. Wadlow's br colt *Jolly Boy*, by Jager, dam Ida, late Anina, late Dahlia, by Hindulah, dam Corybantica, 4 yrs magenta & blk cap
5.—Mr. F. R. Pinkett's *Pinfire*, yrs.........canary, blue sleeves, & cap
6.—Mr. M. Mence's b m *Justice*, by King Lud, out of Astrea, by Adventurer, 5 yrs.......violet jacket and black cap
7.—Mr. E. J. Lewis's bay g *Bonnie Joey*, 4 yrs green, crimson, and black stripes
8.—Mr. H. Lawrence's bay g *Loose Fish*, aged ...violet & white cap
9.—Mr. J. Heywood's bay g *Bounce*, 4 yrs ...white body, & blk cap.

5 15 | THE FROOME HUNTERS FLAT RACE,

Of 30 Sovs. for Hunters. Four-year-olds, 11st.; five-year-olds, 11st. 7lbs.; six and aged, 12st. Winners, once of £50, 7lbs.; twice of £50 or once of £100, 14lbs. Maiden five year olds and upwards, allowed 5lbs. Entrance, 3 sovs to go to the fund. Distance, two-and-a-half miles on the flat.

In 1884 between 6000 and 7000 people came to Bromyard races – by train, by coach or under their own steam. It was a popular day out in the country from Birmingham, Worcester and the surrounding area.

The nine hole golf course was laid out about 1900 overlapping the race-course. The club house is seen on the extreme left.

The three golfers seen below sitting in front of the club house are identified only by initials: E C B, F I B and W E P, but are probably Eustace and Fanny Brierley of Whitbourne Rectory and a friend. Preb Joseph Brierley, their father, was rector there between 1886 and 1913.

T Bowers, Bob Hall, Ted Jones
Standing: Mr Robinson, Jack Partridge, Bill Lock, Dr Hinnings, Bert Turbill, J Woodyatt, T Parkes
Seated: Teddy Jones, Bert Harrel, Parry Hall, Fady Harrel, Bill Harrel, Jim Evans
Danny White, Walter Lewis, Jack James, Eddy James

Bromyard catered for sports for every taste.   Here two victorious teams display their trophies, the Football team, above, in 1910 and the Quoits team, below, who were County Champions from 1908 to 1910.

Standing: —, W Bullock, E Clements, E Page, W Rowberry, J Walwyn, T Watham, J Hinksman, F Billingham, J D Barrs, H G Laister (Hon Sec)
Seated: W Harrell, F James, S R Page (individual champion), W Jones (Capt), A S Allen (Pres), -James (Capt), T Bridgewater, J James, R Baylis

Standing: J Addyman (Umpire), E F H Evans, Rev J B Hewitt, G Rouse, J D Barrs, F Turner
Seated: Rev W Henwood, J E Cuff, Dr P K Lewis (Capt), Rev E A Harrison
W Shuttleworth, J C Custance

There were three clergymen and a doctor in the Bromyard Cricket Club eleven seen here with their umpire in 1905.

It seems that some fine judgement is needed in this bowls match being played behind the Church Institute. The flags on the building suggest that this may have been a special occasion.

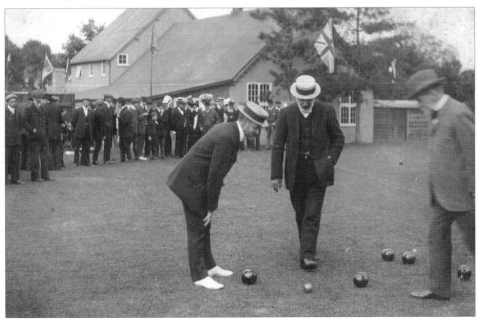

While the men applied themselves to club sports, the ladies donned their motoring headgear and went for a picnic …

… and boys could take off their boots and engage in a serious game of marbles.

Celebration

Back in Market Square on the occasion of another celebration, a few years before Pretoria Day. This is Queen Victoria's Diamond Jubilee in 1897.

A good celebration needs a band and here we have the band of the Bromyard Volunteers (soon to be Territorials) – always mentioned as playing a leading part on any special occasion.

A celebration in the Church Institute, decorated for a special event. The careful arrangement of the tables suggests that this may have been a whist drive.

This large and happy crowd have assembled in the Square to celebrate the coronation of King George V in 1911.

Here we see the band of the Herefordshire Territorials in action. As the soldiers stand to attention, the men remove their hats and the scoutmaster (in the top left-hand corner) is saluting, we must assume that they are playing the National Anthem.

After the formalities the fun begins with a carnival procession through the town.

ACKNOWLEDGEMENTS

All the photographs in this book have come from the Bromyard & District Local History Society's collection. We are deeply indebted to all those Bromyardians and people with Bromyard connections who have, over the years, donated photographs or lent them for copying.

Geoff Gwatkin of Ross-on-Wye has kindly allowed us to use his 1844 and 1998 maps of Bromyard on the back cover. They illustrate beautifully the growth of the town over a period of 150 years.

Most of the information for the captions has come from the Society's publications and its holding of local newspapers. For additional information we have consulted Hereford Library's local history collection and the Herefordshire Record Office.

We would like to thank the Society's Publications Sub-committee for valued advice and encouragement during work in progress.

Orphans Press have dealt with the final preparation with patience and skill.

Finally we must thank the Heritage Lottery Fund for their contribution to this project.

Brenda Allen, Diana Kelly,
Hugh Langrishe, Audrey Lowery,
Mandy Palmer

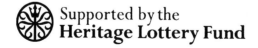

Supported by the
Heritage Lottery Fund